A Stranger's Heart

A Stranger's Heart
Laurence Musgrove

Illustrations by
Myra Musgrove

Copyright 2023 @ Laurence Musgrove & Myra Musgrove
All Rights Reserved

ISBN: 978-1-962148-01-6
LOC: 2023948788
Editor: Reilly Smith

Lamar University Literary Press
Beaumont, TX

for Marie-Clare

Recent Poetry from Lamar University Literary Press

Lisa Adams, *Xuai*
Walter Bargen, *My Other Mother's Red Mercedes*
Christine Boldt, *In Every Tatter*
Devan Burton, *A Room for Us*
Jerry Bradley, *Collapsing into Possibility*
Mark Busby, *Through Our Times*
Julie Chappell, *Mad Habits of a Life*
Stan Crawford, *Resisting Gravity*
Glover Davis, *Academy of Dreams*
William Virgil Davis, *The Bones Poems*
Chris Ellery, *Elder Tree*
Dede Fox, *On Wings of Silence*
Alan Gann, *That's Entertainment*
Larry Griffin, *Cedar Plums*
Michelle Hartman, *Irony and Irrelevance*
Lynn Hoggard, *First Light*
Michael Jennings, *Crossings: A Record of Travel*
Gretchen Johnson, *A Trip Through Downer, Minnesota*
Markham Johnson, *Dear Dreamland*
Betsy Joseph & Chip Dameron, *Relatively Speaking*
Ulf Kirchdorfer, *Chewing Green Leaves*
Jim McGarrah, *A Balancing Act*
J. Pittman McGehee, *Nod of Knowing*
Laurence Musgrove, *Bluebonnet Sutras*
Benjamin Myers, *The Family Book of Martyrs*
Janice Northerns, *Some Electric Hum*
Godspower Oboido, *Wandering Feet on Pebbled Shores*
Carol Coffee Reposa, *Sailing West*
Jan Seale, *Particulars*
Steven Schroeder, *the moon, not the finger, pointing*
Glen Sorestad, *Hazards of Eden*
Vincent Spina, *The Sumptuous Hills of Gulfport*
W.K. Stratton, *Betrayal Creek*
Wally Swist, *Invocation*
Ken Waldman, *Sports Page*
Loretta Diane Walker, *Ode to My Mother's Voice*
Dan Williams, *At the Gates, a Refuge of Milkweed and Sunflowers*
Jonas Zdanys, *The Angled Road*

For information on these and other Lamar University Literary Press books go to www.Lamar.edu/literarypress

Acknowledgments

I am grateful to the editors of the following publications where some of the poems were previously published:

Peregrine Journal
Texas Observer
Voices de la Luna
Pensive: A Global Journal of Spirituality and the Arts
San Antonio Express-News
Amarillo Bay
Inside Higher Ed
The Windhover
Odes and Elegies: Eco-Poetry from the Gulf Coast. Lamar University Literary Press
The Windward Review
riverSedge
Houston Chronicle
Writing Texas
Red River Review
Southwestern American Literature
The Enigmatist
Buddhist Poetry Review

CONTENTS

13 A Stranger's Heart

15 Teaching and Learning

17 So Much Work To Do
18 Sutherland Springs
19 Six Aphorisms
20 More To It
21 Fair
22 Allegiance
23 Freedom Meditation
25 Accommodations Permanence

27 Reading and Writing

29 Hope
30 First Words
31 A New Chapter
32 Reading
33 Single Edition
34 Southwestern University
35 So It Doesn't
36 Words
37 What to What
38 The Plagiarist
39 Thank You

41 Dogs

43 Ready for Tears
44 How to Bury a Parakeet
45 April, Texas
47 Wolves of Dallas County
48 In My Body
49 Backyard San Angelo
50 Waiting
51 Still Here
52 One More Time

53 Texas

- 55 Mourning
- 56 Notes to Self in the Yard
- 57 The Monarchs
- 58 Sunday in the Desert
- 59 November's End
- 60 Toward Carancahua
- 61 Sweet El Paso
- 62 Good Medicine
- 63 February, Texas
- 64 By Far
- 65 After Dark

67 Biography

- 69 I Remember
- 70 Lessons
- 71 Security Check
- 72 Includes Adult Situations
- 73 Heart Sonnet
- 74 Lucille
- 75 Signature
- 76 Hairbrush
- 77 Pore Bearer

79 Fear and Sadness

- 81 Impermanence
- 82 Each Morning
- 83 Basement
- 84 Covered
- 85 Body of Water
- 86 The Dust
- 87 Parade
- 88 Fever
- 89 High Pressure
- 90 Bedtime Q and A
- 91 Codicil

93 Up

- 95 Up
- 96 Who Is

97	Bandage Sutra
99	Fiat Lux
100	Yoga Teacher
101	Black Bean Sutra
102	Slipknot
103	Complexion
104	Metta Guided Meditation
106	Enough
107	Tea Sutra

110 Closing Remarks

111	After Me

113 Words, Images, Collaborations

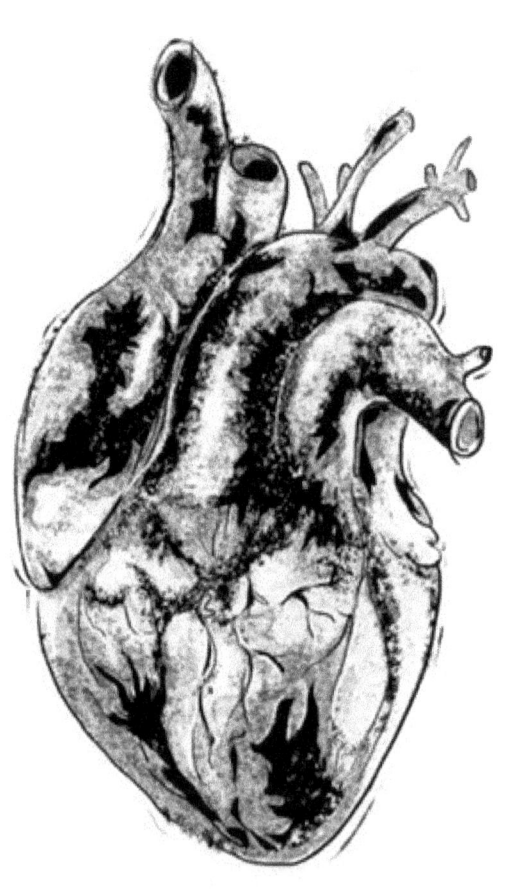

A Stranger's Heart

Nobody makes a mistake on purpose.
Unless the purpose is to make it,
And then it's not a mistake at all
But an experiment into what might
Happen if we tried this or that
So we might learn or feel something
We didn't know before we tried it.
We're all in the mistake-making business,
And the risk to life and limb is what
We're willing to live and be ourselves,
Like deciding to trust a stranger's heart,
Like reaching through this wrought iron
To pet the Great Dane who lives loud
Down the block and sometimes comes
Over to me as I walk home from work
Telling him he's a good boy as I put
My hand on his head risking nothing
Like a mistake I'd ever regret making.

Teaching and Learning

So Much Work To Do

While I was handing out
A poem in class today,
The pages seemed frightened
Of what the students might
Say about them, so they
Held on tight to each other.

I licked my fingertip,
Rubbed it against my thumb,
Peeled away the top page
And handed it to a student
Who said a quiet thank you,
Maybe as afraid as the poem.

Sutherland Springs

Wisdom is lost on the young,
As well it should be.

Let them find it themselves
Along their path, along the stream.

Still, at the very least let me help
Draw their attention to its possibility.

I know I could do better
Than today's class when I went on too long
About the nature of impermanence.

My reference to that recent
Mass murder at a little church

200 miles from here probably
Wasn't a welcome example either.

Six Aphorisms

What we learned before we knew it
Is what we do before we know it.

When you begin to get your back up,
You might begin to back up.

Time is money is what money paid time to say.

A wise ass is a smart ass who stuck with it.

Liars hide the truth out of fear
Because they think their fears are true.

To learn means to have less confidence
In what you know than in what you might.

More To It

It somehow makes me happy
That I'm not the only one who
Has trouble with cause and effect.

I have no idea why my right knee
Sometimes goes weak, except
That I'm 65 and pigeon-toed.

I suspect there's more to it.
And when I took the dogs out
Tonight for their pee before bed,

I saw why it was a mistake
For the birds to build their nests
In the apartment exhaust vents.

Every year, there's a new crisis
On campus. Awhile back, we had
To take active shooter training.

Then later, we learned firsthand
The precipitous rise in student
Anxiety, depression, and panic.

This year, we had the choice
To teach through masks or screens,
If students showed up at all.

When the fledglings were nudged
Out of the nest, two landed hard
On the concrete headfirst.

It doesn't always happen like this.

Fair

> As I did not teach for the good of my fellow men,
> but simply for a livelihood, this was a failure.
>
> "Economy," Thoreau

I've been conferencing with my students
This week on their final papers on Walden.
I've read over their first drafts, seven pages,
Works cited, and they are what you might
Expect: a little awkward, a little unfocused,
A little off topic, a little too personal, a little
Too little. So, when I met with one student
Today to go over his early draft, every time
I pointed to what he needed to revise or edit,
He said, "That's fair." which surprised and
Confused me, as if he was expecting another
Response: accusation, blame, denigration,
A little too personal, a little too, too much.

Allegiance

When I start class with a period
Of sitting meditation and quiet,
I often ask my students to put
A hand over their hearts
So they can feel their chests
Rise and falling with breath,
Their bodies beginning to slow
So their minds know where to go.
And with eyes closed, I go back
To my 3rd grade classroom
With the other boys and girls,
All standing, hands on hearts,
Behind our teacher at her desk,
With liberty and justice for all,
Words we wear out like the knees
In our jeans, the tips of shoelaces,
Braids undone, chewing gum—
Our teacher, too, tattered a bit,
Class after class of us smart-alecks
And do-gooders and scaredy-cats,
Not so different from those here
Who sit with me and pledge
Allegiance to the hearts we got.

Freedom Meditation

Part I
After settling into your posture
With balance and confidence,
Establish a calm and open heart
By breathing through your nose,
Down the back of your throat,
And into your welcoming lungs
Now, focus all of your attention
On the flexibility of your lungs
As they are opening for each breath
And pushing that breath back out again.

Part II
Notice also the front of your lungs
And how your chest is lifted forward.
Then notice how the sides of your lungs
And ribs open widely right and left.
Also notice the bottom of your lungs
And how your belly is pushed forward.
Then feel how your back makes room
For the lungs as they expand behind you.
Notice your lungs inflate in all directions.
Feel also the corresponding contraction
As the lungs naturally release the breath.

Part III
Imagine now that you have two wings
Rooted in your back and shoulders.
They are large yet surprisingly familiar.
You can easily lift and open these wings.
You can easily lower and closer them, too.
On your next inhale, lift and open them.
As your exhale, lower and close them.
Imagine how strong your heart and lungs
And body must be to lift and to open
And to lower and to close them like this.
They have always been your wings.

Part IV
If you stood up and wanted to fly,
You could easily lift yourself from the ground.

Imagine what it would be like to open
And embrace the air around you,
And to take that air and push it down
With confidence and strength as you
Raise yourself up, feet off the ground.
Consider the stamina you would need.
Imagine the freedom and joy possible,
Especially when flying with others.

Part V
When you are ready to teach flight,
Stand across, toe to toe with your student,
And take each of their hands in yours.
Notice and dedicate your attention
To their heart and lungs and breath
And shoulders and back and wings
And to their strength and to their joy,
And also, in their trust in you to forgive
Their fear and awkward beginnings.
Each time they soar in what you taught,
They will feel your hands and release.

Accommodations Permanence

Did you know the word "normal"
Comes from a carpenter's square
Which is an artificial depiction
Of the imagined concept we use
To apply a theory of angles upon
Landscapes, materials, and people
We want to own and command?
So, when I get a series of emails
About student accommodations,
And a paper from a woman who
Volunteers her ADHD as reason
For her lousy object permanence
And time management abilities,
I think, this isn't any "New Normal."
There's nothing to square this with,
Except the oldest curriculum we have—
The ready heart and the open mind.

Reading and Writing

Hope

We rely on others
To make sense of us.

We live in the dream
Of measuring and mistakes.

We could listen better.
We could slow our hearts.

We think too much of us
And never good enough.

We almost see the other
As someone we already are.

We live by what we read
And forget to keep reading.

We want hope from every
Word we never saw coming.

First Words

I'm nothing special
In learning to read
From a hymnal,
Like this one
My mother is holding.
We turn thin pages
Looking for a big number
(And we find it!)
And pointing
To the first word,
She says holy
And again twice Holy.

A New Chapter

> Without empathy on the reader's part, the writer
> can do nothing, . . .
>
> Stephen Dobyns

I led a reading life of books
As I thought writers must lead them:
Underlining passages
So I could return to them later
And follow the crumbs
Back to the house I loved.

Now I'm giving my books away
And sorry for the lines I made
And the words I wrote in the frame
Of the pages that once loved me.
So rarely did I go back and visit,
There was so much new to teach.

Tonight, I am reading for the first time
A chapter for class tomorrow,
And I love this book, too, very much—
But I put my pen down, no more selfies,
Just curious what lines my students
Are drawing on their pages tonight.

Reading

One of the warning signs
Of an approaching migraine
Is the loss of reading.

Each word stands frightened
On its tiny little island.

My eyes are deaf to what
They are calling out to me

And each other as the tide
Is rising up all around them.

Helpless, I close the book
And wait for it to subside.

When it doesn't,
I know I'll be drowning, too.

Single Edition

I'd like to
Read a book
About my books:

A small volume
To brief me again
On what I've read,

Like these piled on
My coffee table
Or bookcased on the wall,

Plus, those at school,
Shelved and aging
Or scattered across my desk.

Also, paperbacks—brown and brittle,
Shared and never returned
(Who knows what's been forgotten?).

It would be slim enough
To thumb each night,
Lamplit as I doze.

This reader of this reader
Will send me back in time,
But return me once again

Trailed by friends
And teachers who said,
You just might find it here.

Southwestern University

When I talked to Gwendolyn Brooks
In Georgetown, Texas in 1973
She was sitting in the student union
Alone in a small dark room to the left
Of the wall of little mailboxes
Where once a month a check came
From my dad that I cashed around
The corner at the post office window
And she was the prize I received
For winning the literary festival
With the first poem I ever wrote
And so it should be no surprise
I didn't even know who she was
And it should be no surprise
She didn't know me either
Which I'm going to say made us
Just about as even as poets
Should ever really want to be.

So It Doesn't

I am trying to hold
This poem together
The best I can
With ink and gravity,
The only heart I have,
And some arithmetic
So it doesn't fall
Into my lap
Like hot ashes
I have to brush off
Onto the floor.

Words

When I read the remembrance
I wrote for my grandmother
At her funeral, I broke down
Too many times, finishing in a sob.

When I sat down in the pew
After my mother's death,
I didn't have the words to explain
How my planet was spinning away.

Now my father is in hospice,
And I'm drafting an obituary
For my brothers to approve,
My heart again a rag in my mouth.

What to What

Every story is about
Our imperfect journey
To perfection.

I can't tell whether
I've learned to be
More concise as I age,

Or I can only handle
A few ideas at a time
Because I've gotten older.

What I fear most is
Watching my memory
Close its door on me.

I can add pretty well,
But I don't always know
What to add to what.

The Plagiarist

I often fail to document my sources.
I confess to copying and pasting my life
Without properly citing the forgiveness
I received from those who raised me,
Unless you can discern in this song
The voice of my mother saying goodnight.

Thank You

I appreciate you deciding you have the time
To follow these letters from word to line to
This line here because I know it's not an easy
Thing to dedicate what little time and energy
We have left to another's thoughts, especially
When you are scrolling down a poem like this,
And like you, I sometimes forget where I am
And have to put things in reverse and return to
Where I lost the trail and that'll take some extra
Gas in the tank that I might not be willing to
Waste again, so you look for something better
To spend your time and energy on, like petting
Your old dog with the same kind of attention
She and her ears have been giving you all day.

Dogs

Ready for Tears

The ghosts of your dogs
Have come to comfort you.
Tonight, you are in bed
Earlier than most nights.
You were ready to turn in
Just after dinner and dishes,
So you decided to kick off
Your shoes and fall into
The sheets and pillows
And covers fully clothed.
The sadness and ready
For tears is coming quickly,
And the ghosts of those
Who knew how to curl next
To you when you needed it
And those who guarded
The door are arriving now.

How to Bury a Parakeet

It's Christmas Day and Millie died.
Nobody knows for sure how she
Came to land on top of her cage
And lay her wings down forever.
Sure, the dogs were watching
Her fly around the room like she's
Flown her whole life skimming
The ceiling and returning again
To her perch or streaking back
Into the door of her cage.
The rituals of keeping a parakeet
Are many to remember and perform
Morning and night exchanging
Water for fresh and new seed
When there's only husks left
On top and the uncovering
And the covering to protect
Her tenderness from the drafts
Drifting in from the wall or window.
But those rituals are now replaced
With the new ones we remember
From planting pets in the garden
And I'm digging a hole behind
The roses thinking about depth
And it's warm enough today
In Texas so the loam is soft
And easily dry enough to dig
A hole just the right size to place
Her into and you burn some sage
And you find a cloth and tear it
To fit and you look at her one last
Time before wrapping up her beauty
And putting her down in the hole
And I drop in a handful of mulch
And a stone and the dogs come
Over for a last sniff and the dirt
Is pulled over her and patted down
And you hand me four more stones
To mark the spot where she rests.
Now the cage is being dismantled
And leftover seed will be poured
Onto the ground on Christmas
As up in the sky and in the trees
There are other birds and melodies.

April, Texas

Today Clementine and I
Are playing with a ball
That I bought for her
From that pile of balls
You might find at the HEB
Loaded up in a tall bin
Across from the bacon
And sandwich meats.
I reached way over
The top for a blue one,
And it was only 1.89
So I thought how easy
It'd be to get another
If she went ahead
And destroyed it just
Like most all the other
Toys we bought her.
Today was also the day
The cedar waxwings
Were passing through,
Stopping off to sing
High in the neighbor's
Stand of pecan trees,
And we looked through
The binoculars to see
Their crowns and yellow
Breasts panting quick
Because they've been
Winging it all the way
From Mexico knowing
Where the berries hang
Ready just for them.
And I kicked the ball
Across the backyard
Like I've been kicking it
For three months now,
And Clem, like always,
Stopped the ball quick
And nosed it this way

And that way around
The yard, and every now
And then she would
Try to bite it, but it only
Scooted away from her.
But not today because
It's gone soft and limp
In the heat and sun,
And she has a mouthful
At last, and you can tell
Just how happy a dog is
By how she runs and runs
And runs and she runs.

Wolves of Dallas County

When sirens raise their call
And ambulances fly through
Our neighborhood, Clem lifts
Her ears, runs to the window,
And wails her location to all
Her ancestry, lost in the dark,
Slid down a ditch, injured
And cold, but then she tilts
Her head at this howler racing
Across the horizon, at what fear
Could make fear run like that.

In My Body

I have a house, a car, a dog,
And a hardware store I like.

When the dog and I take a ride
To buy batteries or sandpaper,
Light bulbs, an extension cord,
Bag of salt thrown in the trunk,

She sits on the passenger side,
Her front paws up on the door,
Her black nose to the window,
Tail wagging to be out and about.

When I have to brake quickly,
I shoot my arm over her way
And put my hand on her back
So she knows to brace herself.

I learned that move in my body
Before seatbelts when my dad
Saved his children from flight
At every surprise and close call.

Backyard San Angelo

Dog barks
At owl for hooting.

Owl hoots
At dog for barking.

There's a lot
Of blame being
Passed around.

Waiting

There's no way
To tell when
A poem will come.
Just like how
A cloud must
Wait to learn
What new color
It will wear
As the morning
Wakes up with
A dog barking
In the distance
Getting ready for
The poem his day.

Still There

When you run your hand
Over your dog's long back
And rub her ears and grab
A paw and shake and take
Your thumb and press soft
Between her eyes and down
Toward her nose and then
Scratch up under her neck,
Your hand gets to collect
All she's done that day:
Each time her ears stood up
And her eyes sparked at
The squirrel in the yard,
Her patience as you fixed
Her dish and her pleasure
As you came home at last
And how she walks so well
Next to you down the street,
The curbs and tires she sniffs,
And how she waits for you
To get in bed to curl up tight
So you can put your hand on
Her again. And when you put
Yours in the hand of a friend
You meet, it's all still there.

One More Time

Excuse me for a brief moment
While I don't make this about
Me or you or the latest trauma
Feeding us through our screens,
But did you happen to see the
Sky tonight, feel how a coolness
Is often collected in the trees
And then set down softly into
Small pockets of relief we get to
Walk through as we follow our
Dogs one more time before bed?

Texas

Mourning

On my first day
In San Angelo, a hawk
Crashed into the asphalt
In the middle of an intersection
Under the bright sky and traffic light
Watching as noon called us to lunchtime,
And feathers like paper were trash in
His talons and bill, as the dove he
Snatched midair felt ribs
Crack and neck snap,
A finale of coo.

Notes to Self in the Yard

The morning is cool
And the best time
To weed because
They usually sleep late
And the long root is loose
And will come out straight
With little practice.

The afternoon is warm
And the best time
To mow because
The grass is dry and proud
And the lawnmower
Can easily whirl its blade
Across its wide flat top.

The evening is calm
And the best time
To stroll along because
The dogs on leash
Will take their time
To linger and sniff
The clean edged curbs.

(See the mockingbirds
Now chasing each other
From yard to shining yard.)

The Monarchs

for Mary Ellen

I for one know what I say isn't new,
But I say it all the same when it bears
Repeating that the only shame we feel
In being ourselves comes from our own kind.
Not from this big sky today nor the tree
That sits under that sky nor the squirrel
Racing after another squirrel around
That tree under that sky wrapping us up
Shameless like the rest of the world we got
Handed to us freely and without gain
To itself in the bargain it gave us.
The monarchs winging it to Mexico
Have no idea how much we cheer them on,
The cricket no ear for our tired old song.

Sunday in the Desert

In the vast parking lot of the new big box church,
Once the vast lot of a furniture outlet gone broke,
Stands a water and ice dispensary circled by cars
And pickup trucks and people waiting at the well.

Jesus had no parable of ice, but here we are taking
Our turn in silence or sharing news about the heat
Holding our plastic jugs and patience and dollars,
Often a quarter left behind in the communion tray.

November's End

Every year, the pecan tree in our backyard
Waits until late November to drop its leaves,
Falling like little yellow boats into an ocean
Of rye I knew to plant just as soon as I saw
The first signs of impending frost and sweaters,
Like the sun following the last of the monarchs
On their yearly visit to our relatives down south.
Tonight, you might also get a wayward whiff of skunk,
And if you look up in that tree, you'll see the very owl
Who once flew so close to me I learned what silence is.

Toward Carancahua

for Randy and Diane

There are two pelicans
Who love each other
And fly outside the rails
Of the highway every day
Spanning Lavaca Bay.
They share a joy
That is only recognizable
As they wing up under
The bridge from below
And pick up the strong
Southeast wind and turn left
To race alongside traffic
Up Texas Highway 35.
Out my passenger window,
I see them eye-to-eye
Before they dive away
Over the chop preparing
To take on another car
Over Lavaca Bay.

Sweet El Paso

When I visit, I expect to drink
Agave beverages
And eat Chile Colorado at L & J's.

On my last trip, I sat at the bar
At Elemi's with a friend
And had rabbit tacos with mezcal.

Upon our request, our host
Showed us our options
And recommended a Rey Campero.

Copper distilled, this espadin
From Oaxaca
Is both fruity and peppery.

After a few sips, I was 6 years old
Watching my mother
Remove her nail polish.

Again and again, she doused
Cotton balls
With sweet, sweet acetone.

Good Medicine

The clutch of fresh tortillas
You bought at Mata's Fruit Store
Just north of the Stanton Street Bridge
Paired perfectly with your green chile stew.

Long ago, I stopped with my daughters
For combo plates and salsa in Las Cruces
And learned the baptism of hatch pepper
As it rinsed the dust from my eyes and soul.

So, when I stood in your small kitchen,
Cubes of pork and potatoes swimming
In a deep stained cauldron of verde,
I knew I was in for another scalding.

After a spoon or two, my tongue lit up
And beads of sweat pooled on my scalp.
Next came tears and laughter, a drippy nose.
Down my neck and back, ran a rivulet.

The mistake, of course, is to lick your lips.
But even that quick blistering subsided
As I peeled back and folded another tortilla
To sop up what remained of my remedy.

February, Texas

If I could tell you the truth
Outside this poem
It would be on a day like this
Here in February
When we open the windows
And the dogs sun
Themselves on the back porch
And it looks like
I need to fill the birdfeeder again
And the sky's the blue
The robin uses to dye her eggs
And I would stand
Next to you in our front yard
As the early weeds
Shoulder their way into the lawn
And I would say
Let's take the whole wide world
Into our arms
And tell it no matter how much
We have loved it
It will never be as beautiful and good
As what's to come.

By Far

When I look up at the sky tonight
(The stars more bright than I remember),
I have no idea how far my eyes can see.

Most people are far smarter than I am,
But they'll never know what I know,
And much of that will be lost anyway.

The worry that darkens my body
Is not so far inside my heart
I can't reach in and take it out.

I want to know if I'll forget first where I am
Or what to do. Or perhaps it will be the names
I've loved this far, like yours, like mine.

After Dark

The Texas I know has
A deep heart and arms
Always open like there's
More than enough room
For everything you need
And everyone in between
And it's like a big black hat
That fits just right on a night
Like this sitting high on Texas.

Biography

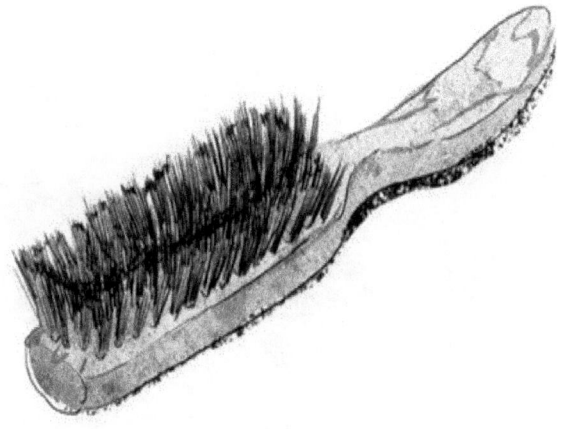

I Remember

for Umpqua Community College

I remember the silver old people who loved me
In the church my great-grandfather helped build.
I remember the nursery school in my grandmother's
Backyard and the swing set and the tall jungle gym.
I remember the classroom speaker above the blackboard
Telling us the president was shot and to go right home.
I remember the teacher in junior high who had to rush
Out of class when blood began to run down her leg.
I remember the high school audience shadowed in the dark
As I sang and danced and tried to remember my lines.
I remember my favorite professor who whispered to us
When she wasn't teaching she was writing poems at home.
I remember the students who put up with me even
When I was still figuring out what they needed most.
I don't remember seeing anyone killed in any of the places
I remember where I loved those who loved me without asking.

Lessons

Given that perfection
Isn't available to us,
We practice and practice
The lessons we're taught,
Even if we've forgotten
Who taught us and why.

My father taught me
How patience works.
My mother taught me
How patience hurts.
I try my patience
When I learn again
The lessons I forgot.

Security Check

"What is your mother's middle name?"
Is the question asked by the artificial
Intelligence of the credit card company
When I log in to check my balance,
And of course, it doesn't know what
Names mean or when she left for good,
Only that it must match what I keyed in
When it asked me to reveal the secrets
It thought it might need to protect me
From those who might want to steal
The very little credit it has allowed me.
And of course, it doesn't have any idea
What happens when I type in "Estelle,"
The name I gave to my daughter as well,
And how I have to stop writing now.
Stars shine because they are crying light.

Includes Adult Situations

I don't know what my life is rated
Or my job or my marriage exactly,
Or my dogs or the car I drive
Or the pecan tree in the backyard
Or the enchiladas I had for lunch,
But I do know adult situations
Is probably just about as precise
A warning as we are going to get
When we sign the mortgage papers,
Decide on burial or cremation,
Unplug the toilet overflow,
Or that time in the city when you bent
Down low on the crowded sidewalk
To pick up the trash others let go.

Heart Sonnet

I can't figure out why I still feel the fear
I first felt when faced with a new doing
I can now do so well. I can still hear
My weak heart singing the halting tune
When I doubted myself and expected blame
From those standing by, expecting the same.
Why is it so easy to see my faults on display,
Blind to the confidence I've already made?
When the life we find is not the life we seek,
The heart builds a memory outside our minds.
We don't get to choose what's buried so deep
Though we get a glimpse in the dreams we sleep.
My father is dying, going deaf, dumb, and blind,
But you can see how loud his heart still speaks.

Lucille

Tomorrow is my mother's birthday
(Two years gone) and I don't know why
It's taken me this long to understand
Who I am because she fell for a man
Who had a way with words (like the man
Who was her father) and I am the man
Who was made by them all and took
The job of the way of words when she
Needed the words the man she fell for
(Or her father long gone) wasn't there
Or when she wouldn't show her tears
(Though I knew) and so became a man
Who fell into the line of men who
Knew who needed words and when.

Signature

When I look for a pen,
I forget to look first in the pocket
Outside my heart where
I put it without thinking, the habit
I learned from my father,
Who wore his pen in his pocket
To reach right-handed,
Like a habit he picked up I suspect
From his railroad dad
Who worked the overnight shift
And recorded the trains
As they passed through Houston,
And my father signed
Checks and letters and contracts
At the business he made
With food companies and grocery
Stores who exchanged in
Coupons and box tops and order
Blanks the women used
To reduce the white rice or tuna
By 25 cents or less or
Get a cat calendar in the mail,
And my dad would take
His pen and sign his illegible name,
A piece of art, a flourish
Of ink, a brag in blue or black,
It made no matter, any
Pen would do, and the cross-
Word every morning
At breakfast, eggs, toast, coffee,
Or he'd just sit and click,
Thinking about who knows what,
Except when he'd draw
The thing he wanted to say, but
Not until he had a pen.

Hairbrush

This morning, you are up early
Because your mind, your daughter,
Who you love has turned on the light
And is sitting on the floor of your bedroom
With the day already begun, and she is reading
All of her favorite books spread out around her,
And you know your mind, your daughter,
Is up for good now, not likely to go back to sleep,
So you get up and pee and wash your hands
And face and dry the last odd dream from
Your eyes, and you pick up her big hairbrush
And sit down behind your mind, your daughter,
And quietly pull her long hair back from her face,
And you say hello and I love you, and you begin
To untangle your mind, your daughter's hair,
And brush it slowly so it doesn't pull or break,
And it is getting smoother and straighter,
And the brush glides, and her hair shines,
And she begins to sing a song you taught her,
And you ask if she wants one braid or two.

Pore Bearer

I know I'm not the sole author
Of my mind and heart. Not even this poem.

Sure, I own this tall container of a person that carries me,
But the contents always leak.

My ancestors jostle around inside me,
And they crowd and shove inside each other, too.

Once, I thought I was a solid hunk of a soul,
Impenetrable, private, my own best man.

But I look at my hands and see my father.
My grin and tears? My mom's.

And who knows where my great-grandmother lives.
My hair, my teeth, my toes, my knees?

I'm going to pretend that she's in the way
I sit on the edge of my bed each morning, bare feet on the floor.

A family tree is not so much a tree
As a river we float on, drink from, drown some.

No matter how much I want to hide from myself,
There's no door to shut, no lock, no key.

The only reason I'm telling you this now
Is to admit to myself that there's no me without you.

I'll also never meet all those I'll live inside. You neither.
But if I return, let it be as a screen door on a warm afternoon.

Some high bird song or tire grumble will be welcomed in.
I'll let the neighbors know what's cooking.

Better yet, Sister, make me a sponge who never tires
Of taking in and giving out and starting again. Pass it on.

Fear and Sadness

Impermanence

The clock on the wall
Has a face and hands,
Parts of our bodies
Chosen for its design
Because they serve as
Our best reminders of
Time's work against us.

Each Morning

Like a bag of ice just out of the freezer,
I want someone to lift me out of bed
And drop me low onto the hard floor,
A good whack to break loose the pieces
Of fear that get stuck together in my heart.

Basement

I have a room at the bottom of my heart
At the end of a long loose pile of stairs
That I stumble down, the only light
Burned out, feeling my way alone,
No idea where the last step is,
But there's no turning back
Until I settle my sorrow
With, *Don't be afraid.*

Covered

I've had colorless mornings
Like you when the bed is happy
To extend our stay at no charge.

Or when the shirt I just
Pulled on must be pulled
Off again and turned around.

How many cups of coffee
Will it take to clear me of
Yesterday's sorrow and selfishness?

I'm not sure what my day would
Be like if not for the loyalty of
My dogs and their ears on me.

Every morning will erase the morning
Before it. When I stand, I wonder if
My knees can still be counted on as friends.

I've opened the blinds as far as
They will go. What more can I
Do to be worthy of this day?

Body of Water

After I was texting
With my daughter
This morning about
Her move to a better
Apartment in Brooklyn,
Especially about her cat
Whose personality
Changed so abruptly,
For the better too,
I began picturing this
Invisible river flowing
Between our bodies,
And by bodies I mean
My body, your body
Her body, animal bodies
All of our bodies,
A river with no source
Other than the bodies
It runs through
Raising our joys and fears
And setting them down
Inside a body nearby.
And sometimes that river
Is calm and slow,
The blue sky reflecting
On its cool flat surface,
And sometimes that river
Is a flash flood.
The rain has been coming
Down so hard for so long
It will break us open,
Rushing out of our mouths,
Our eyes, and every pore.

The Dust

The sadness man
Is here to hand out
The sadness he has.
And we run like
Children into line
To stand to get
Our sadness from
The bag he drags
Up and down our
Street as the dust
Of the sadness
We ran to get just
The day before
Falls from us into
The bag of tomorrow.

Parade

When everyone has a rope
To hold and balance our big
Country high above our heads,
We walk together like nothing is
In our hands or above us at all.

But if we have to march because
There is no rope for us to hold
(See it now starting to float away,
Small in the sky) what do we take
In our hands to bring it back down?

Fever

Where would you like to sit
As you watch the world come to an end?

You remember the fragrant infant halo
Of your daughter's hair and also how

Helpless you felt at her fever and red
Tears as you pressed the cool cloth to

Her head and arms and phoned the doctor
And waited on hold—your broken pleas.

We have called our Earth our mother
So long we've forgotten she's our baby, too.

High Pressure

The weight the morning
The coat the hood the gloves
The wind the street the stranger
The sun the glare the cold
The dog the teeth the fence
The car the exhaust the steam
The weight the morning
The coat the hood the gloves
The wind the wind the wind
The trees the leaves the trash
The stranger the stranger the stranger
The worry the heart the worry
The bed the blankets the night
The bedroom the window the closet
The dark the dark the dark
The pillow the weight the cold
The heart the heart the heart
The morning the weight

Bedtime Q and A

How tall
Is the world?
How thin
Is this moment?

How hard
Was the slap
To your heart
As a child?

We put love
In the arms
Of a future
Who'll hold us.

Codicil

No fear as you
Push me out
Onto the dark ocean
Of my death.

My old boat
May be small,
But the dish of moon
Will be my lighthouse.

Before I drift
Out of sight
Past your forgiveness
And forgetting,

Take this hammer
And yank the planks
From the dock
Of your heart.

Up

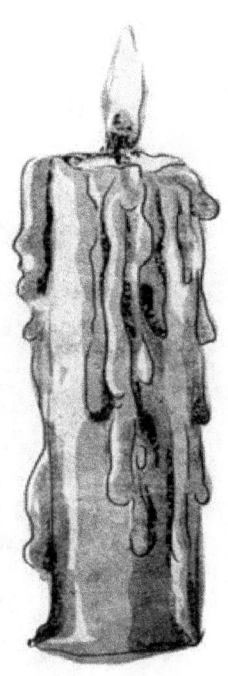

Up

We put the gods in the sky
And then our God too
Because that's where
Our first teachers lived
In the beauty and sun
And wind and clouds,
The anger in lightning,
The peace of morning
(The first art we studied).
We stood upright because
We wanted a better view.

Who Is

When the poem
You want to write
Is about forgiveness,
You begin with what
You can't bring
Yourself to forgive
(The angry mother
The absent father
The daily abuse
Of your heart)
Because you haven't
Yet built enough words
Between you and
The only person you
Should forgive
Who is always you
For not forgiving.

Bandage Sutra

I was emailing the Buddha about how far
I am progressing in my morning meditation,
Feeling like my posture is getting stronger
And beginning to recognize just how my ego
Was shaped by my father and to what degree
My relationship with others and the world
And with myself have been injured by it.

He said, "Imagine your relationship with others
And the world and even yourself this way:
You are covered in sores, all representing
All the ways your ego injures you and others.
Each of these is also covered by a bandage.
So not only are you covered in these sores,
You are covered head to toe in bandages.

You are barely able to move or walk or see
Or hear or feed yourself or even breathe,
Not because of the sores, which are healing,
But because of the bandages hemming you in.
Now it is time to remove these bandages,
But you are afraid to pull them off yourself.
You are also afraid to let others do it for you.

Instead of looking forward to being a person
Without suffering, you are afraid of the pain
It takes to be free of the pain of suffering.
Imagine also now you are surrounded by those
You know and don't know but who are standing
Ready to take a turn at pulling off a bandage,
Each only allowed to remove one at a time.

So they come forward and each asks you
To tell them what the bandage is covering,
And you see they love you, and you trust them,
And you tell them, and before you know it
The bandage is gone, and the next person
Steps forward, and you begin again, and you
Trust this person because you trusted the others.

And this trusting continues until you are able
To hold on to a kind of courage you have
Never felt before while also understanding how
It will stay with you forever, though you still have
Many sores to heal and bandages to be pulled,
Which you find yourself now pulling as well,
Even as others continue to take their turn.

Then you recognize how they have bandages, too.
You ask them about their suffering, their sores,
And before they know it, because you listened,
Their bandages are gone, and they didn't feel
A thing because the pain of healing is not at all
The same as the pain of unnecessary suffering.
Every relationship, even with yourself, is like this."

Fiat Lux

Light never vanishes from the world.
Even in the darkest night, the stars
Glow in their turn, and when the moon
Turns his face upon us (even if it's only
That curved white sail, a ship in the sky),
There's still light up there we can count on.

Sure, there are nights overcast thick
With clouds or rain or falling snow,
But all we need is a good candle flame
Or the lamp beside the bed for comfort.
At my house, I have a nightlight
In the hallway so I won't break a toe.

When God began his work on the world,
He needed some light to find his glasses
And to lay out his plans on the bench
He set up in heaven, pulling the sun close
When he couldn't find the nail or bone
He dropped in the shavings on the floor.

And when he breathed life into all creation
(And this includes you, me, and all we see)
He put a shine on everything he made –
A light with no socket, no plug in the wall,
No cord to trip on, no battery to replace,
A powerful glow no matter how dark.

Still we know what darkness feels like
When without warning or much too soon
The flame we held closest goes out for good,
Never imagining in the life we planned
There'd be a day when the light we loved
Gets buried under shadows and tears.

Times like this, we easily forget a light
Gone missing isn't theirs to take with them.
Because when he said let there be light,
He didn't say maybe, or only if you want one.
It's a permanent gift there's no taking back.
You know how to shine from the shine you knew.

Yoga Teacher

Vriksasana says,
An open door
Stands on one leg.

Tadasana says,
The mirror doesn't
See what it reflects.

Adho Mukha Shvanasana says,
I apologize to the sky
For putting my rear up there.

Balasana says,
I'll save you a place tomorrow
Just like I did today.

Black Bean Sutra

This morning, after cleaning, boiling, and
Resting the beans, I put them in a crockpot
With diced tomatoes, garlic, cumin, oregano,
Onion, paprika, and lots and lots of salt.
I set the temperature on low and planned to
Forget about them for the next five hours.
I then called the Buddha to see if he had
Any plans for dinner, "Salad, beans, rice?"

"Why, yes!" he said, "That sounds good to me.
I always enjoy a dish cooked long and slow.
There's also a tasty lesson in preparing
A meal like this from the simplest recipe.
You and I, like everyone else, arrive into
This world with the same basic ingredients
Slow-cooked in the evolution of our species.
Then, we are slow-cooked again in the family
We inherit, in the places we live, and in the
Habits we learn: such a rich and delicious stew.
It's also the reason for the difficulties we face
When we want to adjust the recipe, when we
No longer enjoy the dishes we've been served,
Those thick juices and flavors we simmer in:
It's so hard to start over, to keep everything tender."

Slipknot

Just a brief reminder here
That the loop of attention
You continuously toss out
Like a lasso to cinch tight
The objects of your desire
Is only a habit of delusion
You learned to perform
From just about everyone
You ever met & raised you—
All schooled in the loud
Pleasure of the self, deaf
To futility's whisper and
Contentment's soft song.

Complexion

> We'll forgive each other
> Till we both turn blue
>
> John Prine

Why forgiveness is blue
And anger is red
And death is white
And why colors bleed
Or hell they do
Is lost on me.

The river that splits us
Is just as surprised as the rain
That you get to have that
Over there
And we have the right
To string you up
Over here.

Like you, I have a long list of regrets:
I pale beside all the people I've failed.

The river enjoys it
When we walk down
To its muddy bank
And think about wading
To the other side.

There's nothing in the sky
That'll hold a line.

Metta Guided Meditation

First, estimate your location, the weight
Of your body, clothed and unclothed,
Sitting or walking or rising up slowly
From kneeling, the architecture of
Bone, joint, and meat, also your skin
Like a container, a gift you unwrap.

May you be safe.

Next, let your ears have a look around.
The air is happy to deliver the music
Of the morning waking and yawning.
(For months, a small tribe of hardhats
Have drilled and hammered and yelled
At each other outside my office window.)

May you be peaceful.

Notice how you haven't been noticing
The way your shoulders are dissolving,
How your breath moves in and out,
Wave after wave breaking upon
The beachfront of your upper lip.
Your ancestors only want to protect you.

May you be kind to yourself.

Your mind may drift into low places,
A fog on the road home you can barely
Drive through, but you are already late
For dinner and your dogs are waiting:
They enjoy without end their surprise
At the light coming out of your hands.

May you accept yourself as you are.

We confuse profit with progress.
It is overcast today, and the trees are bare.
If I could change anything about myself

It would be to listen better to the song
Of my leaving as I sink into darkness.
In what remains: my daughter's eyes.

May you be happy. And may you be free.

Enough

When I'm out of all I can do,
I go into the world to see
Who's outside of what I know
And discover again a land
Of big surprise, and I wonder
How you and I will ever have
The slightest smidgen of talk
Or love in common enough
To hear ourselves agree to
Embrace each other so we
Can whisper the differences
Right out of our hearts.

Tea Sutra

Standing in
The kitchen
This morning
With the Buddha
Preparing tea,
He said,
"The cup
Of awareness
Begins with
A teapot nod
To our ancestors
And a sip
For those who
Would call us
The same."

Closing remarks

After Me

I don't want to fight the world.

Sure, there's much I don't like.
Desire destroys our planet,
And the powerless who bathe
In the dirt and fear all day
Can easily be hidden from view
When the screens big and small
Are paid to show only the angry
And more than one naked girl.
What's new and next will never
Satisfy the mind or the heart
As it breaks against a world
Too heavy to carry or leave behind.

When I say peace, you say it, too.

Notes

Words

Laurence Musgrove is a Texas writer, teacher, and editor. His previous books include *Local Bird*—a poetry collection, *One Kind of Recording*—a volume of aphorisms, and *The Bluebonnet Sutras*—Buddhist dialogues in verse, all from Lamar University Literary Press. Professor of English at Angelo State University, Laurence is also editor of *Texas Poetry Assignment*.

Images

A Brooklyn-based artist, Myra Musgrove's current work explores memoir through various modes, including paintings, comics, and collage. Inspired by Wimmen's Comix, William Morris textiles, and perplexity, she has studied at the Art Institute of Chicago and Studio Art Centers International in Florence. Her latest book is *A Is for Anarchist* in collaboration with American rapper billy woods.

Collaborations

Myra previously illustrated *Local Bird* and *The Bluebonnet Sutras*. They have also collaborated on comics, including an academic article "Drawing is Learning: To Understand and To Be Understood" presented in comic format and published in the *Journal of the Assembly for Expanded Perspectives on Learning*.

Praise for *A Stranger's Heart*

Whether it's a college student, a dead parakeet, a dog that begs walking, or an idea of the heart that needs chasing, Laurence Musgrove tends his subject with deep humility, wisdom, and humor. *A Stranger's Heart* reflects an outlook on the world of compassion, honesty, and disappointment, yet often circling back to hope. These poems intoxicate with their deceptively simple statements and aphorisms clothed in a consistent rhythm of speech in conversation with the reader. Musgrove, always the careful thinker, wonders about some of our most important life concerns such as the influence of childhood on adult life, the inevitability of death, the evil loose in the world, as well as the stunning beauty of our planet. Visit his poems and be prepared to come away with greater insight for living the meaningful life.

Jan Seale, 2012 Texas Poet Laureate and author most recently of *Particulars: poems of smallness*

In these thoughtful and often illuminating meditations on being human, Laurence Musgrove reminds us that "we're all in the mistake-making business": we learn through the risks we take. The risks in these poems all lead to discoveries, and he locates them through precise phrasing and vivid imagery. For the reader, the journey is profoundly rewarding.

Chip Dameron, Member of the Texas Institute of Letters and author of eight books of poetry, including *Mornings with Dobie's Ghost*

www.ingramcontent.com/pod-product-compliance
Lightning Source LLC
Chambersburg PA
CBHW071120160426
43196CB00013B/2643